POINTS OF DEPARTURES

Points of Departures

poems

Paul T. Hogan

White Pine Press / Buffalo, New York

Published by
White Pine Press
P.O. Box 236
Buffalo, New York 14201
www.whitepine.org

Acknowledgments: "Ignorance Toward Fishing" and "Chas Passes" originally appeared in
The Buffalo News. "Fear of Irish Sons," "Of, or From (Mother or Land)," and "Sundays We
Visit (as "Two Poems On Sunday")" originally appeared in *The Legend of Being Irish: A
Collection of Irish-American Poetry,* edited by David Lampe (Buffalo, NY: White Pine Press,
1989).

Publication of this book was made possible, in part, with public funds from the New York
State Council on the Arts.

Cover image: "October #2," detail. Copyright ©2004 by Michael Herbold.

First Edition

ISBN 978-1-893996-23-6

Printed and bound in the United States of America.

Library of Congress Control Number: 2008928423

For those who have come close:
Your influence endures

To Matthew and Lianna
and Barb

With gratitude and love to
Jnmie Margaret Gilliam, Peter Murphy, and Eric Gansworth.
This is yours, too.

" . . . The secret
Of this journey is to let the wind
Blow its dust all over your body,
To let it go on blowing, to step lightly, lightly
All the way through your ruins, and not to lose
Any sleep over the dead, who surely
Will bury their own, don't worry."

—James Wright,
"The Journey"

POINTS OF DEPARTURES

FOREWORD

ONE: HOW WE PROCEED

Two: Fear of Irish Sons

Three: Flopping Magnetic North

Four: Aspects of Departure

Afterword

Foreword

Presence

Upstairs, in the attic of the green
house with white cracking trim
was finished space I called office
with right locations chosen for books,
magazines, and one ashtray, metal,
on the desk, and one of chipped crystal
on the end table made of wide-grained pine.
On this, swollen by slow, wet air,
a line of unconsulted reference books
leaned perpetually to the right.
Irregularly, I went up there — I believed it was good
space to listen — and sat at the desk which faced,
in any rearrangement, the door.

What had startled me was the thief's
failing to close the drawers of the desk
which were so easy to close. More than anything
I may or may not have missed or lost
it was this flap of unfinished business
that threw me, that brought to sharp relief, suddenly,
all the room's marks — Which had I caused?
Which were the business of the dead, the here
and suddenly gone?

And when, days later, I dreamed again,
I went up unrelieved and closed them one by one,
slowly, as though watching for fingers,
puzzling as to whether it would end simply like that,
or start up again or change anything.

ONE:
HOW WE PROCEED

MOVING TO DISTANCE

(Prelude

There are animals — wolves,
some types of birds, I think
cranes — that mate for life.
They move always toward the distance,
circling, or in lines
which are straight or not,
and arrive somewhere
when they stop. They move or stop.
The mate is there, or near, or not.
They are hungry, or not.)

This horse, they tell me at the stable, is named Angel.
Angel, they say, will listen to your voice,
your sound around her neck, and carry you
according to that. She will know
from how you grip the leather strap
whether you can imagine a bit
in your mouth that pulls every direction,
and carry you according to your sense
or lack of sense of that.

And if you let go
the idea there's a path you'll lead her on,
and slacken the reins, and let her move
toward whatever point she's drawn to
in any animal direction,
she'll take you then to places
you'd never find by looking, wanting,
planning for lifetimes ahead.

A Kind of Release

Seeing at times is slow
or however constrained;
the shadows in here,
strange and yellow
crossing the room, take
a long time to stop,
and they are blurred then,
too. I cannot understand
this light, sometimes,
out the window — this glow,
like a fire
at a distance
in the dark
high near the horizon
close to the city.
I cannot understand
how it sucks up the sound,
holds my mouth shut, presses
into my ears. How I don't feel
constrained. How, as I watch,
I can think suddenly,
how muscles slip the blood through
more easily. How the thin
arms of smoke
infiltrate the room,
ease over my shoulders,
calm me,
hold me down hard.

Three Movements at First Spring

1.

The door open. Not widely
so — enough to let
this south-southeasterly
air curl in and spin
planes of cigarette smoke
hung since early November.
They shift like noise shifts
in wind shifting its bearing:
Agitated. Calm. Then spun.

2.

All day, echos of voices — woven
through chatter and the longer
calls of the birds —
have been at me. Like they do in
Liars' Tales of winter cold,
odd words unfreeze
in first spring's air, and swirl now,
freed, seeking their objects,
long since vanished.

3.

All day the voices. Not
constant and intelligent; not
that sound a madman madly seeks.
It's something that bears hearing,
but it's garbled by the wind
like what a lover says in darkness
is garbled by her teeth
just as she turns over,
resettles in her separate sleep.

SLOW STARTING FANTASY, UNCERTAIN END

He offers his back. Stands in the doorway watching
away toward sunset, hears her approach
from behind. Sliding her hands past his sides, she runs
her fingers over his separate ribs, finds
length and tip of each. With his hand set
specifically against the doorframe, he peels back
a splinter, snaps it, wonders if he bleeds,
if his eyes are too dry now to blink.
He realizes the pressure of her hips,
rolling smooth low against his spine,
the trickling of her fingers sweeping randomly
hip to cock to chest. He watches, still, away;
watches how logically clouds move
despite their sway, their changeability, and he wonders
that the butterfly wind of any word now
could cause a hurricane shift by them toward
any unpredictable direction.

A Small Place on the Lake

1. *The Task*

I didn't expect to feel
the lake's restlessness,
standing at its edge
when we arrived. Its tiny, constant
rippling against the banks
was like a stifled wanting
to push beyond its smallness.
It never was at peace.
At twilight, once or twice,
I watched as the too little water
tried hard to catch the whole
of the full moon and the stars
that rose fast so far and away
above it. It managed few,
and only a broken white sheen
of moon's light, the rippling
falling and rising under the dock
like a measure of trying.
I sat with hands clamped, feeling
the small of my back tight,
wanting to stretch, to lend
my white skin to this task
I didn't expect.

2. *Settling*

The bricked-in fire of the cabin's
hearth held us mostly
in its dying out. The logs
we had to burn, crumbling
and cold, heated slowly; the first
weak tongues of yellow flame
leaped and disappeared from behind.
Mostly, it was the dim wait
for the flash point, which came
with sounds like slaps
more than like cracking logs.
Its highest point was reached
just once, for seconds,
then it fell off slow and silent
like a dying fight between
drunk lovers. The lake clapped softly,
smoothing the banks the whole
of the time we recovered, even
when the fire's orange drained
from the windowpanes and we both forgot.

3. *Blackout*

The lights popped out,
and we stopped cold in utter black.
The same black we imagine
the instant of death to be:
our next heartbeat caught
in the handbones of some loose-
robed spirit.

      No such ideas then
as "plan" or "us" or "remember".
Only the waiting for
my heartbeat, my
fingers working toward
anything not black now.
      Then I locked the door,

called to you,
and listened for the water's
birthing slap against the bank
that would force the breath
back out of us.

4. *Waiting for Power*

The lake does nothing
with lights dancing
on its surface — its movement
is beneath those. It's like
the way I see the candle's
flame in front of us,
moving on the mirror of your eye,
and then all the wanting beneath that —
all of it just dark to me.
Once someone showed me
that the surface of the lake
gave the sky's lights a second life:
the first, constant in the high dark;
but then the one that wavers on the lake's face,
divided by my fingers flowing through
like dreams that multiply themselves
the instant they are touched.
Now I think everything must
have two lives: You and I
will always have two lives.

5. *This Storm's Passing*

We are softened to each other,
glad the winds that made us feel
so fragile are pulled away
with this storm's passing.
We pack the car, drive back
from our retreat. And I still don't know
what happens next. Whether

the lull of the city's noise,
in its tidelike rise and fall,
will remind us that the lake's
small motions are not different,
except that here, where we navigate
black asphalt, the sky's lights have just one life:
trapped between black buildings
we forget to look past.

It seems too painless, too, to forget
ourselves; to take as peaceful
the rippling sounds that spread like waves
over the walls of our small place.
Just as it's easy to forget this rain,
streaking the grey faces of glass
after storms pass, was gathered
at the lake, and sent, I like to think,
to revive for lights and for us
our other lives.

We watch the rippling movement
from behind,
from below the surfaces light meets here,
and swirls away or flashes back from.

Hoax of Angels

At dawn birds take stock,
find wings again against light,

duskily call out their survivals.
The boundaries night had stolen,

had given over to crickets, to angels
and their ceaseless, furious messages

the birds reclaim now with their
sharp songs. The trees take hold of,

flip over the wakening wind, and bow
to the west, relaying it away, one

to the next. There: again the birds begin
what had been finished before night's flood.

At dawn, memory's empty, floating up the sky
puffy and slow-blooded, and

the messages of night are lost, turned
into the sounds of birds singing. At dawn,

there were never any angels to begin with.

Three Faces

He fights sleep
the night and
wandering in place,
in his bed, naked, he
lies eyes closed, wide
awake, shaking his foot
quick back and forth or
rocking, up on his side,
arms crossed tight,
a distraction
from sleep, the night
and wandering, bodiless, back
and forth his foot shakes,
the ache
in his shoulders
calms him, holds him
here, he is awake here,
in his sleep, in the night, wandering,
an old woman wandering,
shaking her wrists he
mimics her grinding her teeth,
she too is here,
her eyes closed she reaches the dirt
and lies down she is
naked and young he is
shaking his foot, he is here
she is covered with dirt
and first light and she sings
with his voice and he
rocks, wandering in place,
in his bed, shaking his wrists, calmed
by his physical pain.

How We Proceed

We chose north and drove.
Who goes that way these days?
Who maps directions mile by mile?
It was not to talk specifically
or to arrive. It was to go.
Everything changed as we turned
right and north. The planes of road
and vertices. The sun and temperature.

The lake stopped us,
grey waves curling small and irregular
up on this end of one world. Boats
hung below or above the horizon —
who can say where it is or was? —
or drifted: Left to right,
port, starboard, red or green.
These directions are enough.

The beach was stones, flagged
by the beige stalks of weeds
drained for the season, and we wandered,
breaking through webs and overlays
of ice, turning at random, wordless,
watching the ways our feet fell
and adapted. How we wish our days planned.
How we misread earth's signs.

Two herons stop us. They stand
in a shallow inlet, attentive to each other
for different reasons. One leaps,
and then the other, in slow motion;
they loop wide around us, silent,
straightening and lengthening

as they gather speed, and disappear
with purpose into the grey above,
around, beneath the lake.
Grey and grey and grey.
How we will descriptions.
How we continue.

This Morning

(She moves toward New York)

Susan, I know these mornings
and these trees and the slow way
air moves in hollow rooms
just before day's light
paints. I know this morning
and the inside of this windowglass
streaked by the light
touch of fingertips, slow and mindless,
and the suddenness of lamps
that come on or go off
in washed-out houses
up and down the street.
This morning, and the watched
night that came before; the watched nights
that will follow — into which
others, too, will move, leaving
outlines of last words, echoing
in voices sounding husky, sounding
fluid and without real edge or shadow.

I know this morning and this breath
dreams draw out from us, visions
that drive us out of bed, to the floor
worn down in front of bedroom windows.
How these colors shift, glance to glance
is what draws us back; how
movement has no history beyond
the disturbance of its wake.

                    I know
I've known these separations; this morning
and these choices, these windows
and the way they keep the world
out and muted, and I know now that first light
on this or any morning will refuse
to let a thing alone
to finish taking shape —
to have a single, resolute shadow.

First Frost

Deaf to the shortening
movements of the trees,
I watch them drain and stiffen;
try to put even an echo
of a memorized sound to them.
I raise my hand, fingertips
out, feeling for the air's
turbulence, familiar,
I thought, as rings or gloves
or other fingers slipped
through mine.
But the glass is exact
against the stiff air.
The window is shut now
for months.

North Country, with Loon

I.

Here, it's the Loon
moves the landscape —

the eye across it —
glides down, a wingtip

close enough to water's
surface to break

the tops of ripples
moving across, toward.

Settling in a particular
circle, equidistant

from far and near
shorelines, two

glide in, join twenty.
A third flaps up. Is unsettled.

2.

The body
fills silk well
makes skin frictionless,
a smooth conductor,
porous so that
the oils mix,
the heat of touch
dissipates
to the silk,
the energy without
distraction
flows into,
ripples across
your skin,
widening,
a disturbance
over the lake
of your back,
wingtip of a Loon.

3.

With nothing
of consequence to say —
the past flaps, distant;
wind swirls cold at our backs,
and then warmer —
we lie in the present, wrapped
in thin silk and each other.

Some minutes have walls,
a door to pass through
to the next; it is
a consequence of thinking
all movement is forward.

When we separate,
swing our hot legs to the floor,
the cold air is nearly
astonishing, and we wrap,
standing now, and step
by step like this,
we move in the direction
of the Loon's talk
on the lake: the next moment,
and the next.

4.

We invoke the great loves
of the past; summon them
with specific words
to our ritual. We know
what we're to do: we've chosen
a place, and dressed.

And they come, these
great loves, across time,
or so we can say.
The shudder of the candle's flame:
that's them. They have not altered.
The strain of their passion
is mythological: their eyes closed;
breath rushing into them
and back out.

We dance now to join them.
We say our words, leave tokens.
Even as we move away
an image of us at this instant
stays with them, dancing, removed
from any line of starts or endings.
Look back at them:
even though their eyes show strain,
they dance.

5.

Camera loaded, the light
near sundown blushes
the grey, beat wood
of the boathouse, flashes
along arcs of the waves.
Don't photograph this. Don't render it
immutable now. Let it
distort, let it unravel,
reconstruct itself.
This image will retell
this here and now for years,
without conclusion —
It will never change,
it will always be different,
we will never agree. For now,
let the light slip down
around you. Don't
remember this yet.

6.

What comes
comes. Today
the sun.
Loon's voice
far off
guided me
in dreaming.
What significance?
If it / had led
to you —
Over the
composting leaves,
single direction
not circles
over humps
of hills,
followed it:
Loon's call ...
the pitches
slide up —
a dream
is it?
The sun
behind you
this morning,
your face
a shadow.
You mimic
Loon's talk;
take me
under you.

7.

Again the road. Again
the press of destination,
the demand of arriving.
This traveling is process:
so much to shut out
moving from one place
not home to the next.
You read and dream.
I watch ahead and watch ahead.
So much to anticipate:
the car somehow or me.
Your hand swings over once
and drops up on my thigh;
my charged attention crashes
out from me, a wave up
the skin of your arm.
Startled you look up at me:
I am hard watching ahead, waiting.
Almost brittle.

8.

Memory slips.

The tranquility of this place
is less a lie
than an exaggeration:
even as parts of it fall away —
respecting winter's approach —
it remains a study
in optimism: the return of,
the resplendoring,
the coming back will occur.

Viewing and reviewing
this landscape stretching away,
curling down and away,
the past slips in chunks.
The lake's surface freezes
pint by pint; beneath,
the fishes, the long paler weeds
undulate on the threshold of living.
This tranquility has other names.

Memory slips, the light turns
oblique, the lake is sealed,
and I am at peace with this.
What does not survive
feeds what does. Memory slips;
a next season comes.

9.

This morning I would have sworn
a thousand Loon murmured
in a circle, unbroken around us,
waiting for some sign or motion:
the raising of an arm,
a disembodied word in tongue
closer to their own than ours.
But it was rain,
persistent, wearing away
edges and outcroppings
with immortal patience.
You rose, a pure black movement
across the dark room, spread,
with a finger, the stiff curtain,
and in the seeping light
became eternal an instant,
unperturbed, unpolitic, speechless,
unhuman. A shiver
ran the length of your shoulders
and part of you took flight,
wheeling through that crack, that seam
for safekeeping, and you returned then
to the bed in the less dim room,
ran your tongue lightly
over the edges of my ear,
and murmured something — about rain? —
in no language I could name.

10.

For the half-minute after
I turn the last light out,
the retina opens wildly,
seeking some blush, some
pinpoint of light for balance,
and I move, utterly blind,
toward you in bed, with all
legendary obstacles between us:
the walls, the blind openings
through them, the lakes
of the inexpressible.
I am a journeyman at this.
Slowly through the house,
face up as though reverent,
my fingertips read direction
and lead me to the door
you lie behind. Though you sleep,
your breathing breaks its rhythm
at my approach, and quiets
altogether when I slip, naked
against your back and trace
lightly on your skin the words
that begin all legendary stories:
I have come this far;
I had gotten this close.

Two:
Fear of Irish Sons

Ignorance Toward Fishing

— for Randy

"in hot july
the moon rises out
of the east, the ocean
trips to the shore

to watch

fishermen untangle
seaweed from their lines."

— R. Prus

Not at all what I'd expected: the fish
still hummed and vibrated at the end of the string
though less each time my heart pumped; I, abreast
of my grandfather in the photo, still feel now
what I'd suddenly conceived as the fish's dying
telegraphed up the line to my palm. I'd had no idea
at four or five years old what those practiced motions
ended in. I kept the string straight-arm out
far from my side, and hear now only murmurings
of the praise I'd somehow instigated in those
from whom I'd sought it. I'd felt long before
the weight of the first time's first cast; had dreamed
for days the sight of the line's arc
molded by the wind, perfect from pole's tip
to lead sinker's tail; had even scraped
at flecks of the rod-handle's cork I knew would scale
my deliberate hands. But this I'd had no thought of:
the weight of a life on a thick cord in the hand
jiggling into the air.

SUNDAYS WE VISIT

I. *Visit at One*

My grandfather's bones
and nicotine skin half-step
through uncut spring lawn
back of the state psychiatric hospital,
moored against wind by his final
and first daughter's arm, muttering.
He smiles toothless and thin;
his eyes tint a bright green world
yellow: He watches me look
at my face in them
flashed back to me yellow, and younger

      at home on a snow-muffled night,
parents out, some time before hospital
was home for him, he stopped
at our house for support,
bent to the wind and the yellowing world,
already lost, already lost, his last spark of sense
stunned as I screamed with the force
of a first grandson's terror that I was not
to let him come in,
that Mom told me to send him
back home to wait to be called —
he shuffled away from the twice-locked back door,
struck dumb and blind ...

      When he asks, the third time this visit,
about school, I tell him a joke and his laugh
makes us freeze: while he coughs up his smile, his laugh,
coughs up his sense like a sickness,
his final and first daughter's arm
half-steps him back.

(Interlude — His daughter's Lament:

"There was little left we could do
but let him slip from sanity, from what
roughly in talk is called sanity;
slip from his grandchildren's faces
which he loved but which he lost and regained
one hour to the next. Not silently at all:
he argued, out loud, with his vision
of them standing in front of him,
visiting so they said, wanting to know of him
what, now, he was; what he was saying.
'What is he saying, Mama?'")

(Interlude — His grandson's Lament:

"So yes, bluntly, I believed
he was standing there; that if I woke
fully and looked back
over my shoulder that he would be there;
and in fact, I did, once, look,
not long after so said my mother —
he was there, but by now
I'm less sure how he looked
than how I thought
he would look — and his mouth moved.
Or anyway if he was there
he would try to say something, my grandfather.
'What are you saying, Papa?'")

2. Seven-thirty P.M.

You call with your plan for my evening:
"We must talk," with a dark wash
of drama; "Bring your brother but wait
until after your father is gone."

You have notes on a pad when we enter;
to your left, a vague Chinese man
carved in the lamp looks them over,
grinning at something his painted eyes see.
You keep him close, like a husband.

Tonight, you soliloquize death
while we, your two taciturn sons,
slide an ashtray back and forth between us,
aware mostly you want us to break you

if age chips your senses
or cracks split your patterns:
your life must shatter
with the drama of priceless bone china,
not fade like some painted clay knick-knack
in the dust of a hallway shelf
no one recalls.

TIEIN' YER SHOES

— A Fable of Grandmother

I.

Saints preserve us, child!
Stories you've had and more
are ya wantin'! Yer worse
than ever yer father could be
with yer questions. Take care
with yer jumpin' at life, boy,
lest it jump back while yer tiein' yer shoes.

2.

I was always the soft one
fer chatterin', sure enough.
Yer grandfather cursed it as idle ...
Idle! Fer the love o' God here was I
workin' my hands to the bones,
just askin' a few civil words.

3.

Yer father'd come in with yer grandfather,
not a mumble between 'em,
and straight away off fer a shot 'n a beer ...
to kill off the day ...
smooth out the pain that they felt
from Lord knows what.

4.

We was scared, Paulie.
Scared of losin' our few piddlin' things,
though lose 'em we did and more than once at that.
All yer workin' and scrapin' and fffft! —
Nothin' to show but yer spirit, yer spine,
and the shirt on yer back

5.

It's trouble yer havin' yerself, Son,
plain to see. His thunderin' and cursin' and
always the face of his hand on the back of yer head —
never a chance to get in a word.
It never come easy fer me, I can say.
It never was easy to take.

6.

Stand to him, Son, as much as ya have:
It's what he was taught about bein' a man,
and it sets his mind easy to see ya set firm to his face.
Hate him if you will: Soon enough that'll make little difference.
What he wants fer ya, Son
is fer life not to jump ya
while yer bendin' down tiein' yer shoes.

Fear of Irish Sons

— Of my father's father

I have this notion of you: Irish,
dirt under haphazard fingernails,
a solid stride I suppose. Life,
work, one and the same; humor
at any fool's expense, especially
your own. The flashing hands
of a leprechaun.

There are no pictures. No
black and white snaps of you
curling up on black tagboard;
no comments from my mother, like:
"That's him when your father
was seven or so," or "There he is
outside the parish in Cork —
or would it be Clare?"

My father straddles between us,
silent about you. Isn't it supposed
to make some difference
that I am his first son
as he was yours? He has always
been silent about you.

I etch age into his face. Ruts
that trace the grace of taking on
all comers: no questions, no

foolish twitch for answers.
I drain his hair white. I press his spine
and stoop him over, trying to see you.
I break his knees to sit him down
in a fat, worn chair; drop his forehead to his fingers,
make him just bloody tired.
I fear for my first son.

Passing

— for my mother's mother

Porches are gone from the fronts of houses,
or they're cracked and scratched like worn
leather satchels, uselessly bagging
stray paper and dry leaves, given up
by the prowling breeze. My grandmother

called them "verandas," and bicycles "wheels."
"Put your wheels on the veranda," she'd call
from the top of the steps, waving to shadows
on other verandas, and she'd laugh
with us laughing at her.

Now shadows appear at edges of shrouds
of sheer curtains as I visit the block
where she lived. They sneak into their houses
through doors slyly placed at the sides,
near the back. They spot me as cats do:
with their ears, never their eyes.

Counting cracks in the sidewalk, I pass
at a comfortable pace to the end
of her block, slip into
the smooth stream of Grant Street:

the shrouds of sheer curtains
behind front porch bunkers
sigh back into place when I'm gone.

In Detox

My brother in detox half-learns, alone,
in dark he prefers, the way the body
mutates the no-longer-anaesthetized memory
into anarchy of muscle, of blood, of allegiance.
But my brother, exhausted, misunderstands.
The body does not have language for what it withstands,
and he, in his pale detox cubicle,
desperately makes one sound after the next,
believing that one not yet revealed
will return his body, drugless, to indifference.
What my brother now knows as puking and pacing
and staring without seeing a thing
is what the body turns back of what it's withstood
of the past — This is what detox ceases to calm.
I will talk, he pleads to the walls, I will talk.
My brother, babbling, mislearns: The body, rebelled,
wet in its anguish, cannot distinguish
one oath from the next oath, or
whether or not there will be one.

OF THE FATHER

Do this: Make a statue of him.
Metal or stone, either one. Have it stand
exactly where he stands now,
on the front lawn, home at his back,
mostly on his right. Petition the town
council: get their nod on this.
They won't object. Tell them
it will demonstrate respect
for Americans of stature
who were someplace else first.

Commission a sculptor. Anyone,
but traditionally schooled:
Hard-knocked. Have my father frozen
exactly as he stands now —
in between day and dream.
Have the arms folded over the top
of the stomach, both hands hidden.
Chisel the lips between smile
and frown. Make the head
as if nodding, as if to people passing.
        But glaze over the eyes:
Don't complicate the thing with passion.

My Father, Far In Some Hospital

I startle him with my late
long-distance call,
ringing him back
from his closed-eyed remembering
to the dimmed, sea-green
or bone white room.

"I'm holding up fine ... It isn't
as bad ..." We squeeze our coiled
phone cords with free hands
and he mumbles. I push farther on,
lightly talk around his life, why

he still should rage for it.
Our half-opened eyes roam the blank sheets
molded around him. "Yes,"
he gives in, almost unheard,
"a catheter ..." — in through his groin,
up the fat artery into his wobbly heart.
"I'm too old," he tacks on
through the buzz in the line, and stops,
waiting for me to say:

"Yes. Skip the bypass. Five or ten years
at your more or less age. Maybe a diet,
and stop moving." He breathes out gently:
"Goodnight, love." And gently I rage: "Yes.
Goodnight."

Of or From Mother or Land

These sons
become me,

having bent
me forward

at birth, back-
ward through life;

these sons, these
boys become

me they take
from the first,

the juice of me —
blood, love,

my slickness —
they become

the notes of me
swallowed, they

eat what I sing,
these sons, they

become what
I wish, muscle

of me, spittal.
My luna

their hearts,
their night hearts

yaw, career
in my chest,

the black of them
me; the shine

of them, them,
these sons they

are of me they
become me.

INSTRUCTION

"Pain invents its own language."
— Richard Selzer

You will not understand.
It may be spring, the utterances
of death lost among the loosened trees.
Your ear must ignore much, listen
hard for the low moan
that will offer a way to me.
I will no longer be your mother,
nor you my first son in ways
we have understood. You may
see in dreaming a distant image:
my body arched back
at the shoulders, curved
down the spine in a terrible,
graceless reach for passage,
caught by the heels
in the tangle of some hospital bed
you will have been told is necessary,
is right. Do not wait,
will you. Will you.
Unbind what was me,
cut through those useless heels;
I will be elegant in spite of that
as I fly, instructed
by that awful language.

Sundowning

"Sundowning,
the doctor calls it, the way
he loses words when the light fades."

— Maxine Kumin

He might say to her he's lost
voice, but it wouldn't then be true
if he did. But if he did, he'd add vision,
too: that he's lost all periphery of sight,
his faith for placing in context
that which he sees right

in front of him. He fears
he'll blurt out the lost words
lovers with histories keep covered
beneath the frayed patchwork
of night's quilt. "As they should,"
he mumbles to her senselessly.
               Or
what if he details the dream
of his passing, his literary dying, his release
from having to rename, in daylight,
every small thing from which his nights
drain all recognition, including —

including himself. But with the light now
all but succumbed, and the timbre
of her question long since absorbed
by the blackening trees, he shifts
to give her an answer: "It's nothing ...
Nothing is wrong." —

60

                    And
like diamonds these words
hang from the strand of her interest,
split the last of this light,
circle her sculpted, dark neck.

Semi-Working Still

—— on my father's semi-retirement

You're a poltergeist to them,
you know. An angry, displaced
spirit rattling down distracted
aisles, tapping your annoyance out
on the grey metal shelves
half-empty of stock. "Order
more of this," you convey, scratching
the wall for their attention.
          They are getting used
to it, gathering in circles, re-
living each appearance.
The younger blooded man-
ager mediates, asks "Who were you?
How can we help you
pass from here?"

CHAS PASSES

—for Midge, in memory of Charles

Chas dies in his own bed. Midge, his wife, the city's first married nurse,
guides his passage. She'd had no question how this would turn out.

The beams of the tight cape-cod house he'd built a few boards at a time
settle just enough as his shoulders ease down to let go a soft knock, a sigh.

Deep January, and we've all had too easy a time of it so far this winter.
The hardest came early, braced us for what we were afraid might come,

and we all were ready for worse. There must have been Januarys Chas feared
the wind's cut wind through the walls he'd put up. But as he spent pocketfuls

of change on handfuls of wood week to week, he must have known,
without question, how it would turn out. No matter how white from cold

his fingers would turn, he'd always draft plans to move forward. And always,
through the mess of it, the life in the house would proceed. No matter

finish work yet to be done, next room to rough in. They would be done
as they could be synchronized with the making of lives.

Gaining the peace of the master board after board, Chas took into himself
what journeymen don't yet accept: straight lines are metaphor, square angles

can't be, true vertical is only a notion. He'd smile about that sometimes,
to himself, thinking a house is most solid if given some leeway to shift,

the line of a beam is best laid out to the horizon; a life is well lived
that's approximate to how true we thought it would turn out.

Lower West Side Garden

— *after Milton Rogovin's "Lower West Side Revisited"*

She and I together grew
grey-green vegetables with pale hearts
back of the house, in soil dried
and greyed by soot borne
over the rooftops from streets
on all sides. No waste

equal to that of soil
not put to use. We worked it
as habit, gritty and fine
though it was, blotched
with paper shreds and paint chips
weathered from the house's wall.

Enough we got from it; enough
that we tried. The waste of what we took
we tossed back brittle on the compost;
the pennies that we saved I never
cared to see. Would it matter, money?
Would we not still do this? — one of us
would say. It's enough of a thing
in itself, I'd hear. It was never.
Not this garden. Not this place.

I'd worry, nights, about aphids
cocooning on back sides of leaves,
leeching not so much the plant
would die. Just enough they'd leave
to come back, over and over.
I couldn't spray, stayed by her:
It isn't war, she'd say. Take what's given.
The ground will break again next year.

I'll never hope again
as I did each spring at groundbreaking.
It will be right. Now I've learned,
I'd say, and until the day we broke the ground
for her
she'd shake or nod her head in silence.
And after that the ashen plants
sagged under the weight of my siege,

and the aphids began humming
at night — What other noise
could that be? — and I sprayed.
And now I grow
secretive, as she could be,
and wear grey shades and black, as she wore.
And near sundown, at times,
I bring in stalks of flowers and weeds
to dry, hung at the window,
and I tack them to this wall, as she did.
And they are decorative. And they are dead.

No Repair

— for Pat Sullivan, my father's friend

Your hands shake steadily,
most of your frame, relentless
as a just-wound clock unwinding
on and on to stop. Parkinson's,
whatever that is, already has withdrawn
from you the coiled carpenter's fingers,
the oak carpenter's arms, and, as when
nails are pulled from blind studs in walls
decayed long past fixing, your frame
collapses. There was a time you'd show
a certain glee when the plaster skin
fell and you'd see the task uncovered.
'There's no repairin' that, by Christ.
We'll rip it down and start again.'

Joseph was a carpenter —
How did he die in that story?
Surely to god more mercifully than this
being stripped back to frame, wobbled
to collapse. I'd say pray to him,
but what would he do but step aside
again, pass the prayer along?
He is outside the trinity of carpentry:
make, fix, finally tear down. But
you understand, and it's your calm,
wobbling wait we can't accept.
We are not carpenters.
We can't get past this notion
of fix it again,
start again from here.

It's Patrick's Day Again, Da,

and I've still not got the feel of it. I feel born
to a path already roughed out and my heels dig in to it,
tear up clumps I twist my ankles on. Did you leave there
for some reason close to this?

I hear the Patrick's Day chatter of the isle of emerald,
and I can think only of the pressure
suffered in the forming of it. I see photos
in coffee table books — green wind, green rocks, black
ribbons of wheel tracks mashed into green grasses —
and I think of worms turning over each other
just beneath the soil line.

How could it be otherwise? If not for that churning
beneath, the grasses suffocate, the soil
turns to cracked shale, and the sea
cannot take its pound of shore, day by day by day.

I've not yet got the taste of irish from the glass after glass
I ritually tip today. What does whatever stained your skin
and thickened your back taste like? When you were green,
snapped your knees to the gravel, was the blood
spread over your tongue spiced with it?
When I bleed now, I touch it to my tongue like whiskey:
rare, intoxicating, sometimes sickening.

A vision I had that way was waking:
We were on the far coast of this country, in blinding
spray of breaking waves, and you waded in,
walked in deeper, rowed with your arms. I saw
small fingers hook your shoulders
near the back of your neck, and in this startling, unfamiliar
connection of our skin, I tried not to slip from you,
swimming for Ireland.

Three:
Flopping Magnetic North

INDIANAPOLIS OR WHEREVER

He seeps into my attention
as a camouflaged animal
or insect would: peripherally
something had been registering
faintly in my field of view, and suddenly

I realize he's there, right in front of me,
crouched down on the far side
of the condiment island in the convention center,
reaching beneath it to replenish
supplies for coffee and more napkins and such,
peering up at me from just beneath the table's edge
and just past the long side of the napkin holder.

He looks past me instantly when he sees I see,
as though at something behind me,
above my left shoulder, then quickly begins
whistling a tune vaguely familiar — an amalgam
of tunes or some sort of call more like it —
and distracted completely, I now
try to recall what tune it is, or is trying to be.
Distraction and camouflage.
          My life could take place anywhere

it suddenly dawns on me, and he
would have to be there, somewhere
near me. We live in tandem movement; we are locked
in counterbalance in this life,
traveling this time, and geography
means nothing. Geography
is time's camouflage, a distraction —

(I start to see now as he
picks up his cloth, moves into the field
of tables and chairs
in his absolute territory)

— a distraction I must get beyond
if my soul is ever to get this right,
to be released to whatever
next level of enlightenment. I'm certain this task
he also carries, a faintest dawning of longing
in the back of his head that I feel in the back of my own

and this ritual between us proceeds:
He wipes down one table in four
exact strokes, arranges each chair
exactly at each compass point, and then this table
and these chairs, then this, and these,
this one, and these; with each set complete
he peers at me again, whistling away
in Indianapolis or wherever,
distracted that I've not figured out
the origin of his camouflaged call,
so I can respond
and we both can progress.

SYNCHRONIZATION

The sky is the surface of slate
as it has been long enough
that I have forgotten to keep track
of the day's names. It has grown quieter
out in the air, and cooler.
On days the sun is direct, sounds
travel straighter up, expanding
to warmer, thinner space, only half-heard,
but today they are trapped, ricochet
down from the close clouds and seem
to be clarified, and more directionless.
                    Is it Tuesday today? Wednesday?
I want not to think away from the weather
to chores, or move from the exhausted light
that drops over me through the kitchen window.
Looking away north, between the sharp edges
of two close buildings, toward the stiff mud
fields of Lockport, I can make out
a swatch of far horizon — trees, or the rise
of a hill — squeezed over with grey
from the dropped clouds. Closer to me,
in the middle distance, is a stand of dark trees
whose leaves might color like blood
in clear sun.
                    It's probably Tuesday. Probably
not long into afternoon.

Meditation on the Rise of Zeus from Unsuspected Son to Trickster King

Mostly I move in and out of this meditation
threaded by the steady voice of our guide, who switches
back and forth into languages I know and don't.
My eyes are shut; the orchestrated colors
and cues of the living room are subjugated
to what's left of senses: the refrigerator
tripping off and on, the dog outside,
the coffee beginning to sour from heat

       and Zeus, and Olympus, and the certainty
of one world crumbling, whether in fact
or through the miscues of illusion.
Zeus was servant to the king, his unsuspecting
father Kronos, before becoming king; Rhea's gift
to her son Zeus (in whose place she once used a stone)
was to teach him to be ornamental,
an orchestrated sight that wouldn't distract from
meditation those he meant to overthrow: Kronos,
who stopped thinking at the sight of the boy,
and the Titans, who stopped thinking at the voice of Kronos
and accepted, at the crumbling end, that their world
was no more than the collected miscues
of everything they thought they sensed themselves.

FLOPPING MAGNETIC NORTH

Not home. Not there yet. I'm not
ready to resume the routine of breathing
that air, sweating against the fabrics
of those chairs, that bed. I'm out
and whiskey has flopped my poles; my true
north is south now, and every street
I push toward pushes me away
like wrong ends of magnets pushed at each other.

I can't go home and panic wells up
within me with the sudden flash that
the change won't change back, that
north, inexplicably, will stay south. That
I could lay any compass on every map
I could get my hands on and end up with points
in every direction — useless, drunken, no point at all.

That landmarks are fickle as homes are.
That the poles of this world, over millennia
or within minutes, can flop for no reason
I'd want to hear, and trying to run —
or at least move with apparent purpose
in a direction taken from star and horizon —
may not be a movement away from
as much as a movement against.

FACT

The earth is flat
at twenty thousand feet,
only what I've been told,
what I've been shown
over and over by those
who claim to know what's what
makes me think
I see it bend at the horizon.
Twenty thousand feet
says the captain, over Ontario,
heading across what would be
Lake Michigan on our maps;
toward the bending edge
of as far as I can see.
          Friends of mine live there —
at the edges of what I believe
to be what. They are hungry there
(or so they say), yet they eat so little.
They swipe color up in their hands,
spread it over their faces, yet they wear black
clothes and shoes that are nothing
to the weather. They don't tell me
they live where they do: That's my fact.
When I do not eat, it's for them
out at the edge, and when I mismatch
my shoes to the forecast
it is in tribute to what I think
must be the pain they feel
at insight's constant touch.
          At the edge —
and there is one, always
just off the charts —
I'm certain they know

things I only suspect: like this cannot be
twenty-nine thousand five hundred feet
nor that southeastern Chicago, since
this plane cannot fly, and that smoke there,
looking like clouds, obscuring
the far edge of my sight, cloaks
more than they'll say,
less than I want to believe.

THEORY OF CANVAS AND FRAME

Her finger's skin is canvas,
oils worn in, rubbed, worked,
muted to impressions.

A theory she has
has to do with layer on
layers of paint: one layer on,
then scraped off then another one on;

the surface is fluid, changing
as though by motion of wind
randomly curling up pliable water

like paint. The surface, in theory,
is only diversion for this movement
spread beneath, seeping out to
edges of canvas, paper, water,
and past — and it's here

the work's real act lies hidden:
beneath, beyond what can be stretched
across a single, tenuous frame.

SEVEN POST-MODERN NOVEL NOTES

— for my deconstructive friends

1.

Begin anywhere. Stormy
and dark end-of-May weather,
Friday afternoon; begin
with pulp parody, where
some sharp sound would ring out
now, some mystery insinuate.
Today (that is, present
time): curious, slow-paced,
foreshadowing a phone call.

2.

To or from a Lover.
Tight voice. Insistent,
signifying Need. Say they're unable
to create a viable situation, a scene
to meet at. Disconnect.

3.

More coffee for one of them.
Too much three cups back.
Play out four plot options
here, keep the reader feeling
unanticipated. Or pace and pace
as if gestating thought,
some decision. Blank sheet.
New chapter.

4.

About Literature. Yes. "Writing
is Literature, and that's that."
"Words are not, of course,
'themselves,' but accepted
groups of recollections clustered
around each particular one."
Yes.
No. Strike this.
Wrong for the market.
Blank sheet, new chapter.
Say five or six, figuring
maybe a dozen in draft.

5.

And Five or Six, if not
semiotic per se, should minimally
demonstrate the narrator's,
if not the author's, awareness
that such acts of writing,
necessarily self-
reflexive are ... No.
Get off this. Too prosey
for the form. Break here.

6.

Review in part. The Lovers have discoursed
without resolve. Assume
they're sad, implying restless. Write phones
in dark colors called "expectant."
Have outside look like
an hour past sunset at one-thirty.
The storm should break itself,
move lighter toward June.

7.

The mystery now, foreshadowed.
A little more anyway. Describe
a Lover physically here.
Tiny face-lines dark. Naturally
lit by a south-facing — no, make it
north — dirty window. Have the phone
ring and ring, bring the reader up
to the Lover's eye. Pause.

Warm-Up

It's cold, and dim at eight o'clock
this morning, but she has forced herself
up, slipped on the skin of the dancer,
and now in the grey natural
light of the hall, stretched,
one leg extended back, she uses

heel of palm pushing
hip down more
toward floor, watching
line of body
in mirrors
for signs of
gracelessness.

It has not yet released her, this body; not yet
given over control to the dance, which knows
nothing of floors, only horizons, and nothing
of temperatures except
how thin or thick the air is.

Open-Eyed Dream, In Color

My head pounds like I just made love
drunk, tripping, on speed (hopped up):
unable to come, unable
to let go.

The insomniac crackle of another cigarette,
another cigarette does not soothe;
the wafting smoke rising from the dull,
hot orange tip does not

like a wand in a Disney cartoon,
levitate me magically; does not extract, in a pass,
my pastel-soft soul from my ash-
and-harsh-flesh colored

motionless frame. I could see that:
My half-tone clone soul sitting up,
stepping in short steps
up smoke ropes into clouds,

lifted by strains of Handel's Messiah,
played soft, on kazoos. Then,
at the Gates of Wherever,
my half-tone clone soul,

under a magically poised
cigarette wand whose smoke
comes out sparkling stars,
would pause, soul

of a Disney cliché, and look
back down trembling,
unable to go, unable to come
back to me.

FACE LOOKING DOWN

*"It has always been the fashion
to talk about the moon."*
　　　　　　　　—William Carlos Williams

Now the moon is touched
I want to go there to live.
I will be wary, like a patient
in the grey or mottled light
of a hospital niche. I will wear white
suits, thick and wired, to go out and watch
objects appear in the black sky
whose names and stories will be mine
to conjure. Then make songs in tongues
I will sing mindless and hard
against the air that won't carry sound
away from me. I will turn
my helmet mic off, stand on the moon's mouth,
and while I glare down through the smoked bubble
of my face, toward the greenish and white
mawkish clouds back where you are, I will howl
　　　　"I am your moon now!
　　　　I am your Luna! I have gotten
　　　　away!"
and stomp my light feet,
making the dust glide up.

Caught in a Spanish Coast Cove

At some instant, the gulls fling themselves
off the high, sheer walls of the cliffs
into which the chiseling waves, like the stone
hands of a mason, have cut
this murmuring cove. Yesterday we'd spent
swimming. More like wading, really, entranced,
as though waves pounded out on the sand-
sculpted drum beach the beat to a ritual we knew
we knew. We knew we were watched — the slits
in the faces of the cliffs — and moved
the more ceremonious, facing the sky's heat
with closed eyes, letting our ancient animal shoulders
be pulled down and pulled down to the slowing,
heavy surf.
      That was yesterday and all last night
we shivered at the brooding, chuckling, changing cliffs
that shifted as though they'd been summoned, and chanted
"Morning morning morning" so that they'd freeze
and we could turn our backs. At the first sliver of dawn
we started to climb the cliffs, frenzied to get up
to the inching down line of sun sooner.
      Halfway up from the sand
the gulls fling themselves, screeching like animal suicides,
and the sun blows the wetness of night
from our small, rattled eyes, puts it behind us
as shadows of bodies on faces of cliffs and we sink,
caught in the cliff's frozen cradle.

"There are seagulls over my roof

and over the blue dumpster of the Chinese fast food place," you write,
past which I imagine the Atlantic, cold and roiling off the coast of
Maine, and the wind blowing salt smells and the smells of ripe fu yung, and
you probably deciding whether to move or finish the thought. I wonder
whether the seagulls are caught somehow by the stench of what they scav-
enge, like the way it catches my throat, closing the air off. As they flap
against and over the waves of wind, eyeing the blue dumpster, I think
how much that feels like thinking to me lately: I've had enough of myself;
I'm poking through the detritus of my over and overexamined life, and I
want a truck to haul it away and force me — like the seagulls over your
roof and over the blue dumpster that's empty now — to fly off screeching
in search of other bones to pick, other scraps of rotting nourishment to
flip up in the air and swallow.

BREATH / FOR CREELEY

As in, will it carry?
As in, does it hold up behind

the frame of it, before
meaning, in the way

the chest rises, and falling
puts out the soul? As in

Ellington's Swing, Lorca's
duende, does the breath

fit the body, does it
convey not less

or more a sound's fill
but enough, specifically

enough to slip from talk
to poetry and back

to silence where it doesn't matter
whether it's poetry

or not? Breath
is the work left

to all of us here, to find, specifically,
enough. *(Breath.)* Dig.

Four:
Aspects of Departure

Found Fragments, Transformed

*"...(T)he women, unlike the men, do not idealize the relationships they write about ...
(T)hey do not worship men, nor do they seem to want to be adored themselves."*

— Meg Bogin,
The Women Troubadours

1. *Hesitation*

Seeing you surprises me again.
The voice, your movement, making
the way this place holds back
that much harder.
      What redthroat sings
from one branch more than once?
They rarely do; you surprise me,
I quickly fall still, wonder
how slight a shudder through the tree
startles off the redthroat?

2. *Approach*

At night the roof above is close
and thick and won't let
even a shadow of me loose
with loose hair streaming
that I'd wrap you with.

I keep you blind. You'll hardly feel
my night hair touch you
lightly — so lightly
that you brush it off like cobweb.
Strands of me cling to your glove,
whispering my name
to your back.

Unbound in my room.
From my skirt I spin a wind
that circles you; comes back
to circle me. I am here
with my shifting desire,
beneath the thick roof.

3. *Skirmish*

This visible heart, worn
beating on the sleeve
of a best, worn dress,
is endangered here.
It suffers in the thinness
of this air. It must be covered or
it will suffocate —
I will suffocate —
I cannot draw back in the breath
on which this terrifying heart
came out. Look:
It turns a blacker red, hardens
nearly to a stone the fleetest foot
would twist on in crossing.
Even your skilled foot, love.
Even yours.

4. *Ritual*

In ways, this must have nothing
to do with skin to skin:
Not your hand's dancing
pressure over my breast;
Not my sheathing you.

As here: in this darkness,
we let fall the cloth
that holds our burning in;
release it to the bright hole
the moon is. We are side
to side, a bright, long blade
runs down the bed's center,
each face of it hot
with our heat.

Our hands crossed
over the hard glow of it.
Our fingertips wrapped over
each slicing edge.
The drops of our thinnest
blood, marking out the floor.
The mute, witnessing room.

5. *Impasse*

What is this ugliness in you
that makes me
feel ugly? Are we at the season
touch is covered? Skin hidden?
Is this the season song is bound
within the freezing fingers
of the trees?

Spring will come.
You let yourself forget. You turn —
blind with pride and savage —
to the north, challenging
that intolerant wind.

All who watch are breathless
at the sight of you and wish
to come close. I know their touch
feels hot, but love, it's always brief —
temperamental as spring.
With me the seasons pass.

6. *Leavetaking*

Your words — as ready,
as soothing as your fingertips —
closed my eyes, ran over me.

Each one glided over my skin
fluidly as dreams of my own sleep.
I woke when, wordless, you left.

I will not write. The words I have
breathe out of me and fly,
odd and urgent,

like birds that flap directionless
to an unclear sky.
I cannot stop them on paper,

crumpled in your hand.
But I can be the wind,
odd and blowing back

your light hair. When you lie,
my love, undreaming,
I still will sing of you.

Narcissus' Pond at Night

Narcissus, kneeling at edge,
could not unlock that eye from his eye

as the yellow-white light on his pond-face
blushed into colors of sunset.

Unwavering still when the blush turned red
then flat grey of night, that face

lit by other light, light
distorted, careened off the face of the moon.

At that thin, transforming sight
Narcissus' awe transformed to awe

at the dividing face, the face blemished,
pocked and cut through by the living

and dead things skimming the pond's face;
things from beneath which well up only

in black unreflecting air. And when wind
preceding dawn rippled the image, doubt rippled

into Narcissus, and he no longer could know
which was Narcissus, which eye the right eye

to lock. That was what held him so long that
his knuckles took root through stones at the shore:

not some single true face, but his infinite faces
in wavering light, faces

that pumped blood to his stomach, faces
that never are done.

Body of Men

We cannot be released from them:
they are not traps; the myths
of them mislead. The statue of The Thinker
is straining, not straining to think —
the thought degrades the act and Atlas,
who holds the world up second by second
does not think because to think would be the slip
that brings apocalypse.
                            Hippolyta, Amazon leader, and
each of her warriors in Scythia cut one breast off
in order to draw back and let fly an arrow more smoothly
and understand: it was not in the name of some thought
they cut one breast off: It was to draw back
and let fly an arrow more smoothly.
                            Sisyphus, who strains
for the rest of time against the rock's weight
and the unending rise of the hill
will not be released because he understands
his punishment isn't his endless task; his punishment
is his endless thought of it.

POINTS OF DEPARTURE

I. B___, 1973 — 1976

Whether or not she touched me during those years or whether I touched her I don't now recall. Physically, I mean. If we did, it would have been the touch of boys: staged shoves or backslaps, testing the edges of the ability to control. Whatever it could mean to be a lesbian in those years, she was that, at least in our houses and among faces long familiar to us. Otherwise, her straight brown hair flowed loose to her narrow hips, to the tops of her legs, which I know were too short and I'm certain were too muscular. How could I describe her face other than as handsome?

It was all about sex and it had nothing to do with sex. Physically, I mean. Because we wanted her being a lesbian to mean something real to both of us, we would push at the edges of the constricted, military life we had trapped ourselves into and posture all the ways we'd shake them up if she would not have lost so much to a world that could not, finally, have cared or meant any less. Addicted to pocket-change rebellion, and hash, and speeders, and drinking, we waited for whatever a life 'in the real world' would mean, because whatever it would mean, we would be that.

Once, she tried to ask me something, at her apartment, with her partner H___ watching expectantly. I was vaguely aware of the weight of it in the moment, a point from which we'd change, and only much later did I feel its full press. I did not know. I could not say, though I know I tried hard to get it from her. But the moment broke, and she pushed down whatever they needed of me. Whatever it would have been, I would have been that. I knew somehow that lesbians in such situations trusted boys like me only once, and I knew somehow as well she was astounded we could love.

2. M___, 1982 — 1985

Sex is Art's point of departure: How could I have fathomed that or fathom that white suburban vision had undeveloped sight? Splattered down to my sneakers in the swirl of her movement were wimmin unleashed, wimmin studied, herstories, poems with spittal at the corners of the pages and inconsiderate volume, and a rejection of dance, as I understood it, in favor of movement alone. M___

mostly laughed at me, in a teacherly way I knew I had coming, especially the day I shared that if I were a woman I'd be a lesbian. What I thought that meant was that I'd picked up some vague notion, mostly because of her passion (which is also to say her suffering), of how woman could truly be moved only by woman, and I think I meant I thought that that was better. I'm not sure specifically what it would be better than, just that I thought it would be.

Sex is what waters our thoughts, she'd say, which can also mean it extinguishes, an aspect I had been unable to consider. One can overwhelm the other, which meant (I thought I was starting to see), that at any given moment, one must be chosen. Not dance but movement alone. Not sex but the water of it, spreading out despite attempts to direct it, resisting or succumbing to any act of shaping. Think of raindrops on a window, she'd say. One drop swirls into another and from that point forward both paths are recast. And so, I'd say to her, if I am to fathom this at all (which is also to say grasp), this is the path I should take, and she, spinning out what I still called a dance, would laugh.

3. K__, 1983

Stripped
of everything me
but a likeness
of my white dick
sagging behind
some podium
spewing feelings.
Separatist.
Lesbian.
Radical. She
wanted nothing
of me or
likenesses of me
except whatever
lover I or the likes of me
might have. "Bring her
or them and I'll have come
and hearts in
my hand before
he has time to
finish withering. If you
keep him keep him
away." Startled —
how would I know
aspects of me or my
likenesses should
have been
secreted
before this
company?

4. J__ #1, 1984 — 1992

Art can not only be drawn
out by a delicate or hard touch of fingertips
over skin and into folds of body, but it also
can be spoken aloud. Groups of people
gather to hear this from you, and when I hear,
even though I'm open to the act,
I tip my face down at the thought.

I am unconvinced about confessing. Especially
about how speaking the erotic, which is both light and dark,
and maybe always both at once,
can liberate in either case. Something about this
becomes entangled passing through me. I see
an isolated, unhurried curve of an apparently woman's body,
smell in my mind the arousal, and even think I understand
how this leads to sound and movement free of thought.

But what scares me, sitting among groups of mostly
women who have come to hear you speak all this,
is thinking that I must now accept that
only a woman's body holds this kind of glistening art,
and only the vibration of another woman's fingertips
can fully tease it out and into air.

5. L__ #1, 1993 — 1999

What risk was it to me to believe that her loving this woman
would neither diminish nor deepen her love for me? Think of it
as two flasks, she said, broad and deep at the bottom, rising
to the narrowed neck meant not just to keep back spills
but to keep back mixups. Think further that each fluid
slakes only a specific thirst; one cannot satisfy the need
relieved by the other. Even with this one — and she held
one up — drained completely, this one — and she lifted the other —
full to the top of its throat, could do nothing. Sand to a body
dried in the sun. And if, as you may wish, I were to risk breaking
the one you think superfluous — and here she held one up
at the level of her temple, released and watched it hit the floor
intact, shuddering all the house — this one could do no more
for me than it does now. And I was still uncertain which was which.
        So, I thought, where was the risk?
Was it in my believing her — that she could love me no less
and no more no matter how I or anything might change in any way?
Was the risk in yielding to her way of feeling distinctions
where I felt only singly? Or was the final risk in thinking
I was risking something now that already had been changed,
and therefore lost?

6. C__, 1992 - 2000

I had to come to believe, facing this down,
that sex was no more than two points of departure,
that gender slipped continuously between them,

an ebb, a flow of particulars of feminine
and masculine, the proportions of which shifted
within all of us, dependent wholly on who

or what we faced. I had to imagine
a midpoint, a fulcrum of identity
that you and I traveled near to and away from;

I had to think that we were different
in the same ways. And then I had to feel
that's why you had to love her

in ways that were the same as I.
What threat, then, following this thought,
could I be to myself? If what you did was balance

a part of her because of how you are a woman
and I counterbalanced because of how I am a man,
then we must have finished off each other

in some less visible way, like echoes finish sounds;
or shadows complete forms. And at the end
I couldn't stop wondering at what distance from its source

an echo becomes a sound in its own right?
We must each have been that to her as well,
but which of us was sound and which was echo

had finally to do with which of us she faced
at any moment, and which
she turned her back toward.

7. L__ #2, 1999 — 2000

At twelve-some years
I am in awe of where
we've come to, and in fear. We've left
so many worn guideposts
so far back on this path;
all the directions
I'd been given to follow,
scratched out on ragged scraps of paper,
litter the way behind.
I've abandoned searching common maps
for reassurances, and now just keep moving.

     You have not taken me
toward any point in any distance I have not
also been compelled to move to,
nor I you. The ground
we've traveled has been spongy,
uncompressed, pungent
as our steps sank in
and then were pushed back.

     I've come to understand
that walking ground like this,
ground most people never feel beneath,
leads to ways of seeing that are breath-
taking. And that's also now to say I have
no breath left
to go with you from here.

8. J__ #2, 2001 — Onward

You affirm for me
this fluidity of gender
I'm fixed on
is overrated. You love,
period.
All are welcomed who wish
welcoming; welcoming
what each one
shows and hides
breaches sexual and therefore
other walls obviously
and nearly irrelevant.
We who act as other than
as this or that should act
bring the richness of pain
— which itself is no more
singular than gender
and no less a series
of inventions. Love,
period.

MOVING ALL THE WATER ON THE EARTH

1. *First Phase*

Last night I moved into anger.

How could I have expected to be enough,
to be everything that was needed

as though the moon alone is enough to move every drop of water
in every ocean up and back in tides, day after day?

Can my part not have been that? Have I stupidly thought it
to be larger than it ever could have been?

Can the moon's and my part have been all along to move only some;
to leave what lies deepest, thriving in absence of light,
to be swirled by fingers of untraceable currents that slip in and back

and leave me, the moon, out of it?

2. Second Phase

Tonight I move into silence —
a silence the same as that
of the new moon, which though unseen in a cloudless night sky,
still
renders all the water in all the earth's
depressions

motionless, pushing down gently but wholly
on every surface, masking
all turbulence beneath. How could I have expected

the words of my truth to be enough,
to break from beneath the sheen of all other truths
like a tsunami welling up and pushing back
the moon's bearing down?

The mouth of the face of the moon,
my mouth,
is stretched over with the dark film of this night;
despite the restless motion
of all waves of all oceans,
there is silence:
a gloss over chaos.

3. *Next Phase*

A small edge of one eye of the moon's face is swollen
with the first reflected light of this next, near-final phase,
and this night I move into grief. I have

misunderstood the distance and the closeness necessary
to push and pull the water on all the earth
and beneath your skin and the skin of your dreams,

and so the night sky and your search swallow me.
Should I have kept my part to reflection alone and fallen
still as wind at the moon's rising
while you moved instead, toward me and away?

What is my part now if not to hold still, wait
for the stray light of whatever phase comes next?
                    And how should I move now if not away,
drawing from within you and beneath all the water in the earth
the exhilaration and the terror of life breaking over banks?

4. *New*

Finally I move into full shadow and cannot see my moon face at all
to know what I feel. No one knows how close
or far away I am, and so must guess at whether
the push and pulling they feel
has to do with the moon, with me.

There is a point at low tide, with water pulled away,
when an inlet has no cover; when life within it burrows
beneath sand, or slumps in dry exhaustion,

when why and how all the water in all the inlets
seeps in and then drains over and over
is forgotten in the fierceness of water
bearing witness to movement itself.

How can I believe all this is driven solely by will,
or that life, burrowed into this or that inlet,
will be always exactly the same
each time water creeps back and seeks
another shadowed boundary
bound to be worn away?

Next Room

The man in the next room
and the woman in the next room
of this thin-walled motel have calmed down,
though I wouldn't have said
they'd been all that bad anyway
the brief times their talk rose up loud enough
to carry. Seemed to me things were left out
as voices swelled and then ebbed
like traffic noise from blue highways outside
over and over again towns. Not all words
got said, I could tell — the thickest were clipped,
grabbed back and stashed in a space in their chests
that each of them absently, sensually touched
as the arguing or storytelling went on. Without planning,
they'd started to skim coins and small bills of passion
who knows how long ago — spare change off the top
they'd never tried tracking before. But no more.
Though the words are banged up by the wall,
I hear each of them hedge, all of a sudden suspect
that secrets have piled up between them, accounts
have been padded in order to finance,
not long from last night, a run back to what they recall
freedom is like. And then they stopped telling.
And now I see just how this looks right through the wall:
when he tries to move past her
in the bathroom as she's combing her hair,
carelessly draped in an unbuttoned nightshirt,
his cock slips lightly over the cheeks of her ass,
but he doesn't swell up, and her nipples don't rise
beneath the thin cotton and I see they don't know

what this means, and I try to call out, face to the wall,
having already run as they plan to run,
but I only can weep for the first time in freedom,
albeit without tears, without any sound
loud enough to give me away.

No Message

I know, dialing the number,
you won't be there.
I know because it's Monday,
midafternoon, because the sun is hot,
because the world is in motion
as you will be, as I should be.
It's not my startled voice —
its instantly lost calmness —
or your startled recognition,
some caught word from you
that I want. Not that. There is this ringing
and ringing, this alarm straining
my thickening skin.
                    I want this:
that the telephone rang
in a ring that was mine somehow.
That somehow the sharp echo of the sound
still bounces from wall to wall
when you come in, that the cat is paying,
somehow, closer attention to what you do
because, as you suspect, there's some message
he wants to deliver. I want all this somehow.
You, distracted, searching
the cupboards, checking the back hall,
puzzling over the cat.

Last Gale

A last gale of March leaves us beached
in the muck of spring shorelines; shaken,
relieved to near tears we kneel to take stock,
absently rubbing cramped muscles,
wary for noise of the past in this breeze,
not trusting this calmness to last.

In need of a ritual closing this passage
we form a stiff circle, and with weak song
and gesture, we eulogize those who fought
the same storms, only to break from the strain,
from the clenched grey and cold their forced hearts
harbored for just that much too long.

            Then we stand,
steady weak knees and squint inland
at greening horizons, at sharp rocks
sprouting shadows, at unnamed white mounds
trickling back into black bones of trees.
We decide. We're resolved.

We will turn our torn ships into castaways' homes,
grow bold with new gardens, walk without thinking
back. And in the sand where we beached we'll scrape sundials,
as though they would anchor this setup in time.

AFTERWORD

THE FAMILIAR

— for Barb

Another path can be traveled
in the familiar; one
that leads in a direction
other than contempt,
that encircles a place,
a geography of hard landmarks,
irregular trails known
nonetheless so well that each
footfall fits with the comfort of
ritual, or dance.

And the path can wind to a small place
inside which the body will be draped,
day to day, in such delicate
strands of the ordinary
that the mind's eye will break,
on some particular morning,
its sentry scan of the memorized
horizon, its vigilance for what can
never happen again, and look
away, inward, down — beyond
what may or may not appear
in the distance behind or ahead —

liberated to see
as in a dream
but moving in some way other
than as a dreamer alone.

Author's Note

This work explores feelings of disaffection toward received notions of identity, specifically notions of masculinity, sexual identity, romantic love, and family heritage, in this case, Irish heritage. In all of these, the work seeks points to depart from these received notions, and in that sense, to both expand and refine them.

The work has much of its basis in feminist critiques of culture and identity that emerged through the 1980s, although even those received notions are challenged. It also responds to the attempts to redefine masculinity led by Robert Bly (*Iron John*) later in the same period and into the 1990s. Finally, the work finds its core around the author's experience in his marriage to a woman who ultimately came out as a lesbian after fourteen years together. On many levels, that experience encapsulated all notions of identity and represents the central challenge to all of them.

Ultimately, the work seeks points of return to and ways of belonging within one's various identities. In the same way that gender is far more than sex, all aspects of personal and group identity must be opened, challenged, and greatly enhanced.

THE AUTHOR

Paul Hogan is a native and resident of Buffalo, New York. He spent much of his teens and early twenties working in his family's small office supply and printing business. He left to serve in the U.S. Navy, during which time he was short-stationed for over three years in Spain on the Mediterrean, and then again to pursue writing at the University at Buffalo.

He completed his B.A. in English *cum laude*, left briefly to work in advertising and marketing, and then returned to pursue his M.A. in writing, part of the last class to be offered the writing concentration. On completing his M.A., he accepted the David Gray Fellowship in Poetry and Writing, and worked with Robert Creeley. After two years and the completionof all his coursework toward a PhD., he decided against a career in academia and left to work in the non-profit sector.

Paul has worked for a variety of non-profit organizations in the arts, education, and healthcare He has been actively involved with promoting writing in the community, serving as host and producer of Spoken Arts Radio for PBS station WBFO-FM for over three years, and coordinator of the bimonthly Writer's Cramp Reading series held at Buffalo's Central Park Grill for over six years. He was also director of the Writers-in-Education program for the Just Buffalo Literary Center. While he has done many readings of his work, he has published sparsely.

Currently, Paul is vice president of the John R. Oishei Foundation, a large, general-purpose private foundation providing grants to non-profit organizations throughout the Western New York region, He lives just outside of Buffalo with his wife, Barb, and dog, Jake, and is blessed to have two perfect adult children, Matthew and Lianna.